Mich. Congregational church. Grand Rapids

Grand Rapids Receipt Book

Mich. Congregational church. Grand Rapids

Grand Rapids Receipt Book

ISBN/EAN: 9783743370647

Manufactured in Europe, USA, Canada, Australia, Japa

Cover: Foto ©ninafisch / pixelio.de

Manufactured and distributed by brebook publishing software
(www.brebook.com)

Mich. Congregational church. Grand Rapids

Grand Rapids Receipt Book

GRAND RAPIDS

ℜECEIPT ℬOOK,

COMPILED BY THE

Ladies of the Congregational Church,

—FOR THE—

LADIES' FAIR, HELD AT LUCE'S HALL MAY 15th, 16th, and 17th, 1871.

NEW EDITION,

REVISED AND ENLARGED.

PRICE. $1,00.

PUBLISHED FOR THE COMMITTEE BY H. M. HINSDILL.

1873.

PREFACE.

Several months ago, some of the Ladies of the First Congregational Church in this city desiring to raise some money for a good purpose, compiled a Receipt ·Book.

It met with so large a sale and became so popular that it has been thought best to revise and enlarge it.

Our object has been not to give our friends an *original* Receipt book so much as a *reliable* one. We have nearly doubled in this edition the number of receipts, and they have all been tried again and again by *experienced* house-keepers.

Of course our further object has been to *get* good as well as *do* good. While we may be doing but a very humble work in publishing a Receipt Book, we cannot but acknowledge that much happiness depends on good food well cooked, so we believe this book will *do* good. We *get* good by devoting the profits arising from the sale of it to Christian purposes.

CAKES.

Bermuda Cake.

2 cups molasses, 1 cup each, sugar, milk and butter, 1lb fruit, ¾ raisins, ¼ citron, 1 tablespoon each soda, cloves and cinnamon, 1 nutmeg, 3 eggs, 4 cups flour.　　　　Miss MARY McCONNELL.

Lemon Cake.

1 teacup butter, 3 of sugar, 5 eggs beaten separately, 1 cup milk, 1 teaspoon soda, juice and grated rind of 1 lemon, 4 cups sifted flour.
M. McCONNELL.

Snow Cake.

1½ teacups fine sugar, 1 of flour, 1 small teaspoon cream-tartar whites of ten eggs; flavor to taste.　　　　M. McCONNELL.

Soda Cake.

1 cup butter, 2 of sugar, 4 of sifted flour, 4 eggs—whites and yolks beaten separately, 1 cup milk, 1 teaspoon cream-tartar mixed with the flour, ½ teaspoon soda dissolved in a little water, and put in last; flavor with lemon.　　　　Mrs. W. D. FOSTER.

Raisin Cake.

1 cup each sugar, butter, molasses, sour milk and chopped raisins, 2 eggs, 4 cups flour, 1 teaspoon each of soda, cinnamon, cloves and allspice, half a nutmeg.　　　　Mrs. W. D. FOSTER.

Ginger Cookies.

1 cup each of butter, sugar, molasses and thick milk, 2 teaspoons soda and one of ginger, flour enough to mould—not hard.

Nut Cakes.

2 cups sugar, 1 of sour cream, 2 of sour milk, 4 eggs, salt, and season to taste, 2 small teaspoons soda, flour enough to roll out nicely—not too stiff.　　　　Mrs. W. D. FOSTER.

Rich Cup-Cake.

3 cups sugar, 1½ of butter, 1 of sweet milk, 5 cups flour, 4 eggs, 2 teaspoons baking powder, 1 bowl raisins, citron; keeps a long time.
Mrs. WM. CLARK.

Ginger Crisps.

2 cups molasses, 1 cup sugar, 2 cups butter, 1 tablespoon soda, 2 tablespoon ginger, 1 teaspoon alum.

Miss MARY McCONNELL.

White Cake or Chocolate.

3 cups sugar, 5 of flour, 1 of butter, 1 of sweet milk, 2 teaspoons cream-tartar, 1 teaspoon (small) soda, or 3 of baking powder, whites of 12 eggs.

FROSTING.—Whites of 6 eggs, ⅔ sugar to ⅓ chocolate, put between the layers and on the top. MRS. B. A. HARLAN.

Cookies.

5 cups flour, 1 cup butter, 2 cups sugar, 2 eggs, 1 cup sour cream or milk, ½ teaspoon soda, 1 teaspoon caraway seed or other flavoring. Roll thin and sprinkle on sugar. MRS. H. STEVENS.

Sugar Cookies.

1 cup of butter, 2 of sugar, 1½ of water, ½ teaspoon of soda; flavor with a little nutmeg, almond or lemon, make as soft as possible, roll thin and spread a little sweet milk over each one and sprinkle with sugar. MRS. H. STEVENS.

French Loaf Cake.

5 cups sugar, 3 cups butter, 2 cups milk, 10 cups flour, 6 eggs, 1 teaspoon soda dissolved in milk, warm, 1 nutmeg, 1lb raisins, ¼lb citron; beat the whites and yolks separately.

MRS. H. STEVENS.

Troy Puff Cake.

2 cups sugar, 1½ cup butter, 1 cup sweet milk, 2½ cups flour, 3 eggs, 1 teaspoon cream-tartar, ½ teaspoon soda.

MRS. E. G. GREGORY.

Hickory-Nut Cake.

1½ cups sugar, 2 cups flour, 1 cup raisins, 1 cup sweet milk, 1 cup hickory-nuts, 2 tablespoons melted butter, 2 eggs, 1 teaspoon cream tartar, ½ teaspoon soda. MRS. E. G. GREGORY.

Brides Cake.

1½ cups of sugar, 1½ cups flour, ½ cup butter, ½ cup milk, ½ cup corn starch, 1½ spoon baking powder, whites of 8 eggs, season to taste. MRS. O. S. CAMP.

No. 1. Orange or Lemon Cake

½ tumbler sweet milk, 1 tumbler sugar, 2 tumblers flour, 2 eggs, 4 tablespoons melted butter, 2 teaspoons baking powder; bake in thin sheets, with frosting flavored with one grated orange or lemon.

Mrs. E. G. GREGORY.

Chocolate Cake.

½ cup butter, 2 cups sugar, ¾ cup sweet milk, 2½ cups flour, whites of 8 eggs, 1 teaspoon cream tartar, ½ teaspoon soda; bake in shallow pans.

For the Frosting.—Take the whites of 3 eggs, 3 tablespoons of sugar and 1 tablespoon of grated chocolate (confectioners') to one egg; put the cake together with the frosting.   Mrs. STEVENS.

White Sponge Cake.

1 cup sugar, 1 cup flour, ¼ teaspoon baking powder, add the whites of ten eggs beaten very lightly; bake in a quick oven; flavor to taste.

Mrs. C. B. ALLYN.

Cream Cakes.

6 oz. flour, 4 oz. butter, ½ pint hot water, 5 eggs; boil the water and butter together, stir in the flour while it is boiling; let it cool, then add the eggs well beaten.   Mrs. C. B. ALEYN.

Jelly Cake.

2 eggs, 1 cup sugar, ½ cup butter, ½ cup sweet milk, ½ teaspoon soda in milk, 1 teaspoon cream tartar, in flour enough to make the whole as thick as a good batter; 1 teaspoon flavoring extract.

Mrs. M. L. SWEET.

Delicate Cake.

1 coffeecup sugar, ¾ coffeecup butter, 1 coffeecup flour, whites of 4 eggs.   Mrs. M. L. SWEET.

Mountain Cake.

4 eggs, 2 cups sugar, 1 cup butter, 1 cup sweet milk, 4 cups flour, 1 teaspoon soda, 2 teaspoons cream tartar; flavor to taste.

Mrs. M. L. SWEET.

Sponge Cake.

1 teacup sugar, 1 teacup flour, 1 tablespoon milk with the yolks and sugar, 1 teaspoon baking powder, three eggs.

Miss LUCY SMITH.

Election Cake.

3 cups milk, 2 cups sugar, 1 cup yeast; stir to a batter, and let stand over night; in the morning, add 2 cups sugar, 2 cups butter, 3 eggs, 1 nutmeg, 1 tablespoon cinnamon, 1lb raisins.

Miss LUCY SMITH.

Piccolomini.

1 cup butter, 3 cups sugar, 4 cups flour, 1 cup milk, 5 eggs, 1½ teaspoons baking powder.   Miss L. SMITH.

Soft Gingerbread.

1 cup molasses, 1 teaspoon soda, 1 egg—beaten 5 minutes; add 3 tablespoons water and 3 of sweet milk; stir, and add 1 cup of flour; then add 3 tablespoons melted butter and one more cup of flour.

Mrs. H. S. SMITH.

Pound Cake.

1lb sugar, ¾lb butter— beaten to a froth, 8 eggs—yolks and whites beaten separately, 1lb sifted flour; stir all together, 30 minutes or longer; flavor to taste.   Mrs. SAMUEL JUDD.

Loaf Cake.

½ pint yeast, 3 lbs lard, 5 lbs raisins, mixed with 10 lbs flour; raise over night; in the morning add 3 lbs butter, 6½ lbs sugar, 18 eggs. nutmeg, mace and cinnamon; raise 2 hours, then add ½ cup cream or milk, with teaspoon of soda dissolved in it; bake in slow oven. Makes 10 loaves, and will keep all winter.

Mrs. SAMUEL JUDD.

Stonington Cake.

3 cups sugar, 2 cups butter, 5 cups flour, 1 cup milk, 4 eggs, 3 teaspoons baking powder, 1 nutmeg; fruit as you please.   Makes 2 large loaves.   Mrs. E. E. JUDD.

Another kind of Cookies.

1½ cups sugar, ½ cup butter, 1 egg, ½ cup milk, 1 teaspoon soda, 2 teaspoons cream tartar, spices.   Mrs. C. B. ALLYN.

Bread Cake.

5 cups raised dough, 3 cups sugar, 2 cups butter, 1 cup sour cream, 3 eggs, 1 teaspoon soda; mix well together, and if necessary add more flour; flavor to taste; add fruit if you like, very nice.   Mrs. C. C. ROOD.

Fried Cakes.

2 quarts of flour, 1 cup of sugar, butter the size of an egg, 1 egg 1 pint sweet milk, 2 tablespoons baking powder thoroughly mixed with the flour.   MRS. O. S. CAMP.

Queens Cake.

3 cups white sugar, 1 cup butter, 1 cup sweet milk, 6 eggs, 2 teaspoons cream tartar, 1 of soda, or 1 heaping teaspoon baking powder in 4½ cups sifted flour. This quantity will make 2 cakes, one of which can be made into a jelly cake. Flavor with lemon.

Mrs. O. S. CAMP.

Crullers.

1 egg, 1 tablespoon melted lard, 1 tablespoon sugar ; mix hard, roll thin ; cut in squares with slits to run the fingers through ; fry in hot lard. You can increase the quantity as many times as you like.

Mrs. O. S. CAMP.

Cape Ann Berry Cake.

4 cups sugar, 1 cup butter, 1 quart sweet milk, 1 tablespoon salt, 2 teaspoons baking powder, 5 pints whortleberries, or other berries ; flour to form a thick batter ; to be baked in a dripper : cut in squares for the table, and serve with butter for tea.

Mrs. WM. M. FERRY.
Grand Haven.

New Haven Loaf Cake

8 lbs flour, 6 lbs sugar, 3 lbs butter, 1 lb lard, 10 eggs, 1 quart milk 1 quart yeast, ½ pint brandy, ½ pint wine, 1 ounce mace ; mix flour, lard, yeast, eggs, brandy, wine, and 1 quart of sugar together, and let it rise. When light, add with the other ingredients 2 lbs citron, 2 lbs raisins, 1 lb currants. After it is raised the second time, without stirring the mixture, put into pans as carefully as possible ; allow it to stand a few moments before putting it into the oven. (Most excellent.)   Mrs. WM. M. FERRY,
Grand Haven.

Imperial Cake.

2 cups pulverized sugar, ½ cup butter, ⅔ cup sweet milk, 3 cups of flour, whites of 8 eggs, 2 cups of seeded raisins chopped and dredged with flour, 1 heaping teaspoon baking powder in the flour, 2 teaspoons powdered mace, the meats from 1 lb of english walnuts broken in quarters. First put in your dish a layer of cake, upon

that a layer of raisins and then a layer of nuts; stir raisins and nuts not mixed lightly into the remainder of the cake; fill dishes and bake. Mrs. O. S. CAMP.

Frosting.

Whites of 4 eggs, 1 lb powdered white sugar, lemon, vanilla or other flavoring; throw a small handful of sugar on the eggs soon as you begin beating, and keep adding at intervals until it is all used up. Icing made in this way will dry in two hours.

Mrs. O. S. CAMP.

Eureka Pound Cake

1 lb sugar, 1 lb flour, ½ lb butter, 6 eggs beaten separately, 1 cup sweet milk, 1 teaspoon soda in the milk, 2 teaspoons cream tartar in the flour, flavor to taste. Mrs. O. S. CAMP.

Lemon Cake, No. 2.

2 cups of sugar, 2 cups of flour, 4 eggs, ½ teaspoon salt, 1 heaping teaspoon baking powder; bake in sheets with the following mixture spread between each layer. The grated rind and juice of 2 lemons, and the whites of 2 eggs beaten with ½ cup sugar. Mrs. O. S. CAMP.

California Loaf Cake.

2 cups of butter, 3 cups brown sugar, 1 cup sour milk, 5 eggs, 1 teaspoon soda, 3 tablespoons cinnamon, 2 cups raisins, 1 cup currants. Mrs. O. S. CAMP.

Temperance Gingerbread.

1 cup molasses, 1 cup sour cream, 1 egg, 1 teaspoon soda, 1 teaspoon ginger: make about as thick as cup cake.

Mrs. O. S. CAMP.

New England Ginger Cake.

1 cup butter, 2½ cups brown sugar, 4 eggs, 1 tablespoon ginger, ½ glass tart cider, ½ cup sour milk, ½ teaspoon soda, 4 cups flour. To be eaten warm. Mrs. PIERSON,

Ionia.

Gingerbread.

1 cup molasses, ½ cup butter, 1 teaspoon soda dissolved in ¾ cup boiling water, 1 teaspoon ginger, 1 teaspoon cinnamon, 1 egg; do not stir stiff, and bake slow. Miss ALICE J. FRALICK.

White Cake with Eggs.

1 cup butter, 2 cups sugar, powdered, 4 cups flour, 1 tumbler new milk, 1 teaspoon soda, 2 teaspoons cream tartar, whites of 6 eggs flavor with mace. Mrs. PECK.

Hickory Nut Puffs.

2 tablespoons flour, 2 oz. melted butter, 2 oz.,sugar, 2 oz. hickory nuts, 1 small teaspoon baking powder.
Mrs. II. D CARPENTER.

Coffee Cake.

1 cup cold coffee, 1 cup sugar, 1 cup molasses, 1 cup raisins, ½ cup butter, 5 cups flour, 1 teaspoon soda, allspice and cinamon.
Mrs. JUDD.

Delicious Cake.

2 cups sugar, 1 cup butter, 1 cup milk, 3 cups flour, 3 eggs, ½ teaspoon soda, scant teaspoon cream tartar, stir butter and sugar together, and add the beaten yolks of the eggs, then the whites; rub cream tartar in the flour last thing. E. E. J.

Cocoanut Cake.

1 cup butter, 2 cups sugar, 3 cups flour, ⅔ cup sweet milk, whites of 8 eggs, 1 teaspoon cream tartar, ½ teaspoon soda, 2 tablespoons whisky; bake in thin cakes; put together with a thin frosting of grated or descicated cocoanut; sprinkle cocoanut on the top.
Mrs. J. B. WILSON.

Almond Cake.

1½ cups sugar, ½ cup butter, 2 cups flour, 1 cup almonds, whites of 4 eggs, ¾ cup sweet milk, 1 teaspoon cream tartar, ½ teaspoon soda; bake on square tins. Mrs. GEORGE JUDD.

Lady Cake.

1 cup sugar, 1 cup flour, nearly 1-2 cup butter, whites of 5 eggs; flavor with almond and bake in flat pans. Mrs. FARMER.

Olive Gingerbread.

2 cups molasses, 1 cup sour cream, 1-2 cup butter, 5 cups flour, 2 teaspoons soda, 2 teaspoons ginger; bake about as thick as cup cake. Mrs. FARMER.

Vanilla Cake.

1½ cups sugar, 1½ cups flour, ⅓ cup corn starch, ½ cup sweet milk, ½ cup butter, 2 teaspoons baking powder, whites of 6 eggs beaten stiff; stir the butter and sugar together until creamy; 2 teaspoons vanilla, last thing before baking; mix thoroughly.

Mrs. E. M. KENDALL.

Union or Custard Cake.

2 cups sugar, ½ cup butter, 3 cups flour, ½ cup sweet milk, whites of 6 eggs, ½ teaspoon soda, 1 teaspoon cream tartar.

For the Custard—1 cup sweet milk, ½ cup sugar, 2 tablespoons corn starch, yolks of 4 eggs; when cold flavor with vanilla. To be made in layers, with custard between, like jelly cake.

Mrs. E. M. KENDALL.

Cream Cake.

Break 2 eggs into a teacup and fill with cream, 1 cup sugar, 1½ cups flour, 1 teaspoon cream tartar, ½ teaspoon soda; for the inside, 4 eggs, 1 quart sweet milk, 1 cup sugar, ½ cup corn starch, flavor with lemon or vanilla. Miss PHRONIA ROOD.

Fruit Cake.

1 lb dry flour, 1 lb sweet butter, 1 lb sugar, 3 lbs stoned raisins, 2 lbs currants, ¾ lb sweet almonds blanched, 1 lb citron, 12 eggs, 1 tablespoon allspice, 1 tablespoon cloves, 2 tablespoons cinnamon, 2 nutmegs, 1 wineglass of wine, 1 wineglass of brandy, 1 coffeecup molasses with the spices in it; steep this gently twenty or thirty minutes, not boiling hot; beat the eggs very lightly; put the fruit in last, stirring it gradually; the fruit should be well flavored; if necessary, add flour after the fruit is in; butter a sheet of paper and lay it in the pan. Lay in some slices of citron, then a layer of the mixture, then of citron again, &c., till the pan is nearly full. Bake four or five hours, according to the thickness of the loaves, in a tolerably hot oven, and with steady heat. Let it cool in the oven gradually. Ice when cold. A very small piece of soda, about as large as a pea, and the same of amount salts of hartshorn, improves this cake. Mrs. DON G. LOVELL.

White Mountain Cake.

The whites of 4 eggs, 1½ cups sugar, ½ cup of butter, ⅔ cup sweet milk, 3 teaspoons baking powder, 2 cups flour, flavor to suit the taste.

THE FROSTING—Whites of 4 eggs, a little tartaric acid, a teaspoonful of lemon extract, pulverized sugar to thicken; to be made in layers with frosting between, like jelly cake.

Mrs. L. E. PATTEN.

Cookies.

3 cups flour, 2 teaspoons baking powder, 4 eggs, 2 cups sugar, 1 cup butter.

Mrs. L. E. PATTEN.

Doughnuts.

2 eggs, 1½ cups sugar, ⅔ cup sweet milk, 2 teaspoons baking powder and a pinch of salt, flour to thicken.

Mrs. L. E. PATTEN.

Cream Cake.

1 cup of cream, 1 cup white sugar, 2 eggs, a little salt, 1 teaspoon soda, 2 cups flour.

Mrs. JOHN W. FRENCH.

Mt. Holyoke, Mass.

Fruit Cake.

6 eggs, five cups flour, 2½ cups brown sugar, 1 cup of molasses, 2 cups butter, 1 cup wine, 2 teaspoons soda, 1 lb currants, ½ lb citron, ½ lb raisins, nutmeg and cloves to taste, enough to make it look dark and spicy.

Mrs. JOHN W. FRENCH.

Mt. Holyoke, Mass.

Pound Cake.

1 lb butter, 1 lb sugar, 1 lb flour, whites of 10 eggs, wine-glass of wine, 1 teaspoon baking powder; flavor to taste.

Mrs. L. E. GRANGER.

Gingerbread.

1 cup molasses, 1 cup sugar, 1 cup sour milk, 1 cup butter, 3 eggs 4 cups flour, 1 tablespoon ginger, 1 teaspoon soda.

Mrs. L. E. GRANGER.

Water Cookies—No Eggs.

1 cup water, 1 cup butter, 2 cups sugar, 1 tablespoon baking powder, flour enough to roll out.

Mrs. L. E. GRANGER.

Sponge Cake.

4 eggs, 1 cup Sugar, 1 cup flour, 1 teaspoon baking powder; flavor to taste.

Mrs. L. E. GRANGER.

Grand Rapids Sponge Cake.

Take a gill cup, (not a gill measure.) 2 cups pulverized sugar, 1½ cups flour, 8 eggs, the yolks and whites beaten separately and very light; flavor with lemon juice and a little of the rind grated. Makes two loaves very nice.

Sugar Cookies.

1 cup butter, 2 cups sugar, 2 eggs, ½ cup sweet milk, ½ nutmeg, knead soft and roll thin.   Mrs. J. MORGAN SMITH.

Ginger Cookies.

1 cup sugar, 1 cup molasses, 1 cup butter, 1 egg, 1 tablespoon vinegar, 1 tablespoon ginger, 1 tablespoon soda dissolved in boiling water.   Mrs. J. MORGAN SMITH.

Chocolate Cake.

1 full cup butter, 2 cups sugar, 3½ cups flour, 1 scant cup milk, 5 eggs, leaving out the whites of 2, 3 teaspoons baking powder.

Make frosting with whites of 2 eggs, 1½ cups pulverized sugar, 2 teaspoons vanilla, 6 tablespoons grated chocolate; bake in one square shallow tin, and put frosting on top.   Miss F. Mc QUEWAN.

Sponge Cake.

1 lb eggs, 1 lb sugar, ½ lb flour. Beat the yolks and sugar very light, also the whites separately, then add the flour stirring it very little; add the rind and juice of a lemon.   Mrs. C. H. JOHNSON.

Lemon Jelly Cake.

1 cup sugar, 4 eggs, butter size of an egg, 1 cup flour, ¾ cup sweet milk, 2 teaspoons baking powder.

JELLY FOR CAKE.—1 cup sugar, 1 egg, 1 large apple grated, 1 lemon grated, beat together and cook till quite thick.

Mrs. SILAS K. PIERCE.

Soda Pound Cake.

3 cups sugar, 1½ cups butter, 4½ cups flour, 1 cup sweet milk, 7 eggs, 3 teaspoons baking powder: flavor to taste.   Will keep fresh a long time.   Mrs. S. K. PIERCE.

Crullers.

4 eggs, 8 tablepoons sugar, 4 tablespoons milk, 6 tablespoons butter, 1 teaspoon baking powder.   Mrs. L. E. GRANGER.

Tea Cake.

1 egg, 1 cup sagar, 1 cup milk, 1 tablespoon butter, 2 cups flour, 1 teaspoon allspice, 1 teaspoon baking powder.

Mrs. L. E. GRANGER.

White Sponge Cake.

Whites of 5 eggs, 1 cup flour, 1 cup sugar, 1 teaspoon baking powder; flavor with vanilla.   Mrs. L. E. GRANGER.

Delicate Cake.

1 cup butter, 2 cups sugar, 1 cup milk, whites of 8 eggs, 4 cups flour, 1 teaspoon baking powder, flavor to taste.

Gold Cake.

Use the same receipt with only ½ cup butter, and the yolks of the eggs.   Mrs. L. E. GRANGER.

Patent Tea Cake.

Sift 2 teaspoons cream tartar and 2 tablespoons white sugar into 1 quart of flour, beat 2 eggs, add after melting a piece of butter the size of an egg.   Mix all with a pint of milk, and the last thing a teaspoon of soda dissolved in a little milk : bake in muffin rings.
Mrs. S L. WITHEY

Ginger Snaps.

2 cups brown sugar, 2 cups molasses, 1 cup shortening of any kind, but if fresh add a little salt, 2 teaspoons soda, 2 teaspoons ginger. 3 pints flour to commence with, rub shortening and sugar together into the flour, add enough more flour to roll smooth, very thin. and bake in a quick oven. The dough can be kept for weeks, and bake a few at a time.   Mrs. JOHN. W. FRENCH,
(The best rule in twenty.)   Mt. Holyoke, Mass.

Tea Cakes.

2 teacups flour, 1 teacup milk, 2 eggs, 2 teaspoons cream-tartar, 1 teaspoon soda, 2 tablespoons sugar : bake in rings or gem irons.
Mrs. OLCOTT.
St. Louis, Missouri.

Dough-Nuts.

2 eggs, 1 cup sugar, ½ cup butter, 1 cup milk, 2 teaspoons baking powder, a little salt and spice, nutmeg or cinnamon. flour enough to knead soft, and roll.   Mrs. ROLLIN CLARK.
Bunker Hill, Ill.

Raised Cake.

2 cups of raised dough, 1½ cups sugar, ¾ cup butter, 3 eggs, 1 teacup raisins, stoned and chopped, cinnamon and nutmeg. ½ teaspoon soda disolved in little water.
Mrs. G. G. LOVELL. Spring Lake.

Tumbler Cake.

3 eggs , 1 tumbler raisins, 2 tumblers currants, 1 tumbler sugar, 1 tumbler molasses, 5 tumblers flour, 1 tumbler butter, 1 tumbler sweet milk, 2 teaspoons soda, spice to taste.

Mrs. G. G. LOVELL, Spring Lake.

Bread Cake.

2 cups light dough, (hop yeast) 2 eggs, 1 cup sugar, 1 cup raisins, ½ cup citron, ½ cup butter, 1 nutmeg, ½ wine glass brandy, 1 teaspoon soda; stir all well together, add a little flour; let stand half an hour before baking.

Miss FLORA CADY.

PUDDINGS.

Salem Pudding.

3½ coffee cups flour, 1 cup molasses, 1 cup sweet milk, 1lb stoned raisins, small piece suet chopped fine, 1 teaspoon soda, 2 teaspoons cream tartar, 2 teaspoons ground cloves, ½ teaspoon salt; steam 3 hours; eaten with sauce.　　　　　Miss MARY McCONNELL.

Whortleberry or Blackberry Pudding.

3 cups flour, 1 cup molasses, ½ cup milk, 1 qt. fruit, 1 teaspoon soda, dissolved in as little water as possible; boil in a mold 1½ hours; sauce.　　　　　Miss MARY McCONNELL.

Sunderland Pudding.

1 pint milk, 6 heaping tablespoons flour; 6 eggs—beaten separately; sauce.　　　　　Miss MARY McCONNELL.

Indian Pudding.

1 pint sweet milk, 1 teaspoon soda, ½ cup molasses, 2 cups Indian meal, 1 cup flour, raisins or currants; steam two hours; sauce.　　　　　Miss MARY McCONNELL.

Eve's Pudding.

6 oz. grated bread, 6 or 7 chopped apples, 6 oz. sugar, 6 oz. currants, 6 eggs, 6 oz. chopped suet, nutmeg to taste; boil 3 hours; sauce.　　　　　Miss MARY McCONNELL.

Troy Pudding.

1 cup suet, 1 cup milk, 1 cup raisins, 1 cup molasses, 3 cups flour, 1 teaspoon soda; steam two hours.　　　　　Mrs. E. G. GREGORY.

Cold Corn Starch Pudding.

1 quart boiling milk, 3 tablespoons corn starch mixed in cold milk, the yolks of 5 eggs, with 5 tablespoons fine sugar; let it cook a few moments, then pour into a buttered dish and set in the oven to brown; beat the whites to a froth with 3 tablespoons of powdered sugar, and put on top; flavor with vanilla.

Mrs. S. L. WITHEY.

Rice Pudding—Without Eggs.

2 quarts new milk, ½ teacup rice, 1 teacup raisins, butter size of a butternut, 1 teacup sugar; season with nutmeg; bake two hours.

Mrs. NOAH STEVENS.

Christmas Plum Pudding.

1 ℔ dry bread or crackers, 1 ℔ chopped suet, ¼ ℔ citron, ¼ ℔ candied orange and lemon peel, 1 ℔ raisins, 1 ℔ currants, 8 eggs, 1 pint milk if needed, 2 nutmegs, 1 tablespoon pounded cinnamon and mace mixed, ¼ ℔ sugar, 1 tablespoon salt, 1 gill brandy: mix very dry; boil six hours.

SAUCE FOR ABOVE.—1 ℔ powdered sugar, ½ ℔ butter, 1 large glass wine or brandy, whites of 2 eggs well beaten ; set in a warm place one hour before eating.   MISS MARY McCONNELL.

Huckleberry Pudding.

1 pint molasses, ½ teaspoon soda stirred in molasses till it foams, 3 pints berries, flour as stiff as you can stir, a little cloves and cinnamon ; steam four hours.   MRS. S. L. WITHEY.

Steamed Pudding.

1 cup sweet milk, 1 cup raisins, 1 cup molasses, ½ cup butter, 3 cups flour, ½ teaspoon salt. nutmeg or cinnamon ; steam 2 hours.   MRS. S. N. GREELEY.

Sunderland Pudding—Another Kind.

1 pint cream, 4 spoons (large) flour, 6 eggs, a little salt, butter the dishes and fill half full ; may be baked in cups; to be eaten with maple syrup. cream and sugar. or any thin pudding sauce.   MRS. N. L. AVERY.

Queen's Pudding.

1 pint bread crumbs, 1 quart milk, 1 cup sugar. the yolks of 4 eggs, beaten, the grated rind of a lemon, butter the size of an egg ; bake until done but not watery; whip the whites of the eggs stiff and beat in a cup of sugar in which has been stirred the juice of the lemon ; spread over the pudding jelly or sweetmeats, and pour over it the whites of the eggs; replace in the oven and bake lightly ; eat cold with cream.   MRS. N. L. AVERY.

Nantucket Pudding.

1 quart berries, or any small fruit. 2 tablespoons flour, 2 tablespoons sugar ; simmer together and turn into moulds ; cover with frosting as for cake, or with whipped eggs and sugar, browning lightly in the oven ; serve with cream.   MRS. WM. M. FERRY,
        Grand Haven.

Boiled Indian Pudding.

3 cups of meal, 2 cups flour, 1 pint sour milk, ½ teacup molasses, 3 eggs, teaspoon salt, tablespoon butter, teaspoon soda; boil 2 hours.

Mrs. L. E. GRANGER.

Cream Pudding.

1 pint cream, yolks of 6 eggs, 6 tablespoons flour, ½ pint milk, 1 tablespoon sugar, little soda and salt; rub the cream with eggs and flour.

Mrs. C. B. ALLYN.

Plum Pudding—Without Eggs.

Take 2 pounds of bread crumbs, sift through a calender, 3 tablespoons flour, 1 lb brown sugar; mix thoroughly; then add 1 lb suet chopped very fine, 1½ lb raisins stoned and chopped, 1 lb currants, ¼ lb citron cut in small pieces, ½ oz. ground allspice. Having mixed all well together, moisten with a little ale or milk, press the mixture into the bottom of a basin well buttered, fill to a trifle above the brim, spread some flour on the top, and tie over a wet cloth. Place the pudding in boiling water and boil five hours.

Great care is required in all puddings of this kind, not to make them too wet, or they will be heavy.

Mrs. BREWER.

Baked Indian Pudding.

2 quarts milk, 12 tablespoons Indian meal, 2 eggs; take part of the milk and scald the meal in it, then add the cold milk, then eggs; then sweeten with molasses and sugar to your taste; butter the size of an egg, cut in bits a little nutmeg; eat with hard sauce or thick cream sweetmeat.

NEW ENGLAND.

Plum Pudding.

1 cup raisins, 1 cup currants, 1 cup suet, 1 cup sour milk, small teaspoon soda, ¾ cup sugar, 1 teaspoon cloves, 1 teaspoon cinnamon, ½ nutmeg, flour enough to make thick as cake; steam 2 hours; sauce of butter and sugar.

Mrs. PIERSON, Ionia.

Suet Pudding.

1 cup of suet chopped fine, 1 cup molasses, 1 cup sweet milk, 3 cups flour, 1 egg, ½ cup raisins, 1 cup currants, 1 teaspoon soda, 2 teaspoons cream tartar; spice to taste; steam three hours; put raisins in bottom of dish; serve with liquid sauce.

Mrs. JOHN THOMPSON.

Spring Lake.

Orange Pudding.

4 oranges, slice in small pieces, 1 cup sugar into 1 quart of nearly boiling milk, stir 2 tablespoons corn starch and the yolks of 3 eggs; when cool, mix with oranges; make frosting of the whites for the top.   Miss ALICE J. FRALICK.

Queen's Cranberry Pudding.

1 cup of milk, 1 egg, piece of butter size of an egg, 1 teaspoon soda, 2 small teaspoons cream tartar, flour enough to make a stiff batter, 1 cup cranberries; steam one hour; serve with liquid sauce.
                                                        PHRONIA ROOD.

Tapioca Pudding.

3 tablespoons tapioca, 1 cup sugar, 1 quart milk, 3 eggs; boil $\frac{3}{4}$ of the milk, wash the tapioca, and stir into milk; boil a few minutes, then add the rest of the milk, the yolks of eggs, and sugar; bake; when cold cover with jelly, then add the whites of eggs beaten with little sugar; set in oven and brown.   Mrs. L. D. PUTNAM.

Chocolate Pudding.

1 qt. sweet milk, 3 oz. grated chocolate; scald the milk and chocolate together; when cool, add the yolks of 5 eggs, and 1 cup sugar; bake about 25 minutes; beat the whites for the top, and brown in the oven.   Mrs. C. B. ALLYN.

Almond Pudding.

2 quarts milk, boil and stir in 2 heaping spoons of flour; let it boil and stir to keep from burning; cool it and stir in 6 beaten eggs. Take the skins of 2 lb almonds, pound them fine and stir in salt, sweeten and flavor to taste. When put in the oven add lumps of butter on the surface.   Mrs. HOLLISTER.

Porter House Pudding.

1 teacup rice, 3 pints milk; set the pan into water and let it simmer until soft, stirring all the time; sweeten and flavor with vanilla, and put in the oven to bake.   Mrs. J. B. WILSON.

Apple Pudding.

Layer of sliced apple, seasoned with sugar, butter, &c., then a layer of bread crumbs, 1 cup water, apples last; bake and eat with sauce, or sugar and cream.   Mrs. J. S. CROSBY.

German Puffs.

1 pint milk, whites of 8 eggs, yolks of 6, 5 tablespoons flour, 1 tablespoon melted butter, a little salt; bake in cups half full, for 20 minutes; serve with sauce as follows: Whites of 5 eggs, beaten to a froth, with a coffeecup of sugar, and the juice of 2 large oranges.

Mrs. H. J. HOLLISTER.

Frost Pudding.

½ teacup rice, 1 quart milk, stand it in water and cook till soft; 3 tablespoons sugar, yolks of 4 eggs, grated rind of 1 lemon, stirred with the rice and milk; the whites beaten to a stiff froth, with 4 tablespoons powdered sugar, and spread over the top; stand in the oven to brown. Mrs. J. B. WILSON.

Lemon Pudding.

1 cup sugar, 1½ cup milk, 1 grated lemon, yolks of 2 eggs, white of 1 egg; bake in pie paste.

FROSTING.—White of 1 egg, 4 tablespoons powdered sugar.

Mrs. FARMER.

Snow Pudding.

To ½ box of Cox's gelatine put ½ pint cold water, after this is dissolved add the juice of 2 lemons and ¼ lb. sugar, and 1½ pints boiling water; let this stand until cold; beat the whites of 4 eggs to a stiff froth, adding one tablespoon sugar, spread this over the jelly.

SAUCE.—Scald 1 pint milk, beat the yolks of the 4 eggs sweeten, and add grated rind of the 2 lemons; stir into the boiling milk.

Mrs. FARMER.

Plum Pudding.

1 cup suet, chopped fine, 1 cup molasses, 1 cup milk, 1 cup raisins, 3½ cups flour, 1 egg, 1 tablespoon each of cloves and cinnamon, nutmeg, a little salt, 1 teaspoon soda; boil three hours in a pudding mould set into a kettle of water; eat with sauce. Mrs. PECK.

PIES.

Lemon Pie.

1 coffeecup sugar, 3 eggs, 1 cup water, 1 tablespoon melted butter 1 heaping tablespoon flour, juice and little rind 1 lemon.

Miss MARY McCONNELL.

Lemon Pie.

1 lemon, 1 cup sugar pulverized, ½ cup water, 1 tablespoon flour ; chop the lemon after paring and pressing out the juice ; 3 eggs : beat the yolks and sugar well together, then add the chopped lemon, juice, water and flour ; do not use the rind. Reserve the whites of the eggs and after the pie is baked spread them over the top, beaten lightly, and return to the oven until it is a light brown.

Mrs. W. D. FOSTER.

A Trick Worth Knowing.

Pie crust can be kept a week, and the last be better than the first if put in a tight covered dish, and set in the ice chest in summer, and in a cool place in winter, and thus you can make a fresh pie every day with little trouble. Mrs. MATHEWS.

Mince Meat.

To 4 lbs. of boiled fresh beef chopped very fine, add 4½ lbs. chopped apples, 4 lbs. brown sugar, 2 lbs. butter, spice to your taste ; moisten with cider or currant jelly reduced with water. If cider is used, and is quite tart, add a cup of molasses and scald.

Mrs. L. S. LOVELL, Ionia.

Frosted Lemon Pie.

1 cup sugar, 1 cup cold water, grated rind and juice of 2 lemons, yolks of 4 eggs and white of 1, 1 tablespoon flour, flavor ; bake and then add whites of 3 eggs, beaten to a froth, with 1 cup sugar, spread on top. Mrs. M. L. SWEET.

Cocoanut Pie.

½ cup desiccated cocoanut soaked in 1 cup of milk, 2 eggs, 1 small cup sugar, butter size of an egg.   Mrs. N. D. CARPENTER.

Another Cream Pie.

Whites of 3 eggs, beaten to a stiff froth, 2 tablespoons sugar, 1 cup cream with milk to fill the plate : bake in one crust.

Mrs. C. B. ALLYN.

Summer Mince Pie.

2 eggs, 3 rolled crackers, 1 cup sugar, 2 cups molasses, (a little less,) ½ cup butter, ½ vinegar, 1 cup hot water, 1 teaspoon each, spices, raisins, &c.   Mrs. L. D. PUTNAM.

MEATS.

Spiced Beef.

Take the lank of beef and rub in a great deal of salt and pepper; roll it up as tightly as possible, tie with a stout cord firmly ; boil as you would corned beef; when cold slice for tea.

Mrs. S. L. WITHEY.

Potted Pigeons.

Clean and stuff with onion dressing, thyme, &c.—do not sew up—take 5 or more slices of corned pork, let it fry awhile in a pot so that the fat comes out and it begins to brown a little ; then lay the pigeons all around in the fat, leaving the pork still in ; add hot water enough to partially cover them; cover tightly and boil an hour or so until tender ; then turn off some of the liquid, and keep turning them so they will brown nicely ; then heat and add the liquor poured off; add extra thyme, pepper, and keep turning until the pigeons and gravy are nicely browned, and served with the gravy poured over them.

Miss MARY McCONNELL.

Baked Fresh Fish.

Clean the fish, stuff it or not as preferred, cut very thin slices of pork and lay on the outside ; skewer on the pork and bake.

Mrs. HARVEY.

Veal Loaf.

3 lbs. veal chopped very fine, butter size of an egg, 3 eggs, 3 tablespoons cream or milk, mix the eggs and cream together ; mix with the veal 4 pounded crackers, 1 teaspoon black pepper, 1 large tablespoon salt, 1 large tablespoon sage ; mix well together and form into a loaf, bake 2½ hours, baste with butter and water while baking.

Mrs. E. E. JUDD.

A Swiss White Soup.

A sufficient quantity of broth for 6 people, boil it; beat up 3 eggs well, 2 spoonsful of flour, 1 cup milk; pour these gradually through a seive into the boiling soup, salt and pepper.

Mrs. J. B. WILSON.

Pressed Turkey or Chicken.

Boil the fowls in as little water as possible (salting a little) till very tender, take out the bones and take off the skin, chop and season with pepper and salt and piece of butter; tie in a strong cloth and press with heavy weights. Mrs. S. L. WITHEY.

Chicken Salad.

A pair of chickens, ½ lb. melted butter, 1 pint rich sweet cream, yolks of 10 or 12 eggs boiled hard, 1 teaspoon of cayenne pepper, 3 tablespoons English mustard, 1 tablespoon salt, celery according to taste, 1 pint vinegar or ½ pint according to strength; mix the eggs, mustard, pepper and salt all together, then add the butter, and lastly the cream. Mrs. C. ALFRED SMITH.

Reading, Penn.

Another kind of Chicken Salad.

Take a chicken weighing about 3 lbs., boil tender; when cold, remove the bones, chop fine using both dark and light meat, boil 4 eggs hard, rub the yolks fine with 2 teaspoons mustard and 1 teacup thick cream, salt and pepper to taste, chop the whites of the eggs, and as much celery as you have chicken; the last thing add 1 teacup of vinegar. Mrs. C. C. ROOD.

Fish Salad.

Take a fresh white fish or trout, boil and chop it fine, put with the same quantity of chopped cabbage, celery or lettuce, season the same as chicken salad. Mrs. EGGLESTON.

Mrs. HOVEY.

Chicken Cheese.

2 chickens boiled tender; chop them, but not too fine; season with salt and pepper, boil 3 or 4 eggs and slice them; line moulds or dishes with these; pour in the chicken and add the liquor they were boiled in. When cold slice for lunch or tea.

Mrs. JOHN W. FRENCH.

Mt. Holyoke, Mass.

Beef Omelette.

4 lbs. raw beef chopped fine, 4 rolled crackers, 4 eggs, piece butter size of an egg, season with pepper, salt and sage; make 2 loaves of this, roll them in crackers, and bake; slice when cold; very nice.

Miss FANNY McQUEWAN.

Baked Beans.

Take 2 quarts white beans, pick them over the night before, put to soak in cold water; in the morning put them in fresh water and let them scald, then turn off the water and put on more, hot; put to cook with them a piece of salt pork, gashed, as much as would make 5 or 6 slices; boil slowly till soft (not mashed) then add a great spoonful of molasses, ½ teaspoon soda, stir in well, put in a deep pan, bake 1½ hours. If you do not like to use pork, salt beans when boiling, and add a lump of butter when preparing them for the oven.

NEW ENGLAND.

Frizzled Beef.

Shave dried beef very thin, put it in frying pan, add milk or water, when hot stir in a tablespoon of flour wet with cold water and 3 eggs, stir until thick, and dish immediately.

Mrs. J. MORGAN SMITH.

Plain Omelette.

Beat 6 eggs slightly with chopped boiled ham; put a piece of butter size of a butternut into a frying pan; when melted pour in the egg; when half done, double turn-over fashion, cook over a moderate fire. To be eaten immediately.

Mrs. J. MORGAN SMITH.

Potatoes Fried.

Pare and slice the potatoes thin, cut them if you like in small fillets, about a quarter of an inch square and as long as the potato will admit; keep them in cold water till wanted, then drop them into boiling lard; when nearly done take them out with a skimmer and drain them, boil up the lard again, drop the potatoes back and fry till done; this operation causes the fillets to swell up and puff out; sprinkle with salt, and serve very hot.

Mrs. J. MORGAN SMITH.

Mock Cauliflower.

Take white crisp cabbage, boil in salted water until tender, drain off water and add a little milk, boil up again and season with butter, salt and a little pepper.   Miss PHRONIA ROOD.

Beef Hash. (Prof. Blot.)

Chop cold roast beef, or pieces of beef steak; fry ½ an onion in piece of butter; when the onion is brown, add the chopped beef; season with a little salt, pepper and nutmeg; moisten with the beef gravy if you have any, if not, with sufficient water and little butter; cook long enough to be hot, but no longer, as much cooking toughens the meat.   An excellent breakfast dish.

Mrs. J. MORGAN SMITH.

French Oyster Pie.

Having buttered the inside of a deep pie plate, line it with puff paste or common pie paste, and prepare another sheet of paste for the lid; put a clean towel into the dish (folded so as to support the lid) set it into the oven and bake the paste well; when done remove the lid and take out the folded towel; while the paste is baking, prepare the oysters; having picked off carefully any bits of shell that may be found about them, drain off the liquor into a pan, put the oysters into a stew pan with barely enough of the liquor to keep them from burning; season them with pepper, salt and butter; add a little sweet cream or milk, and 1 or 2 crackers rolled fine; let the oysters simmer, but not boil, as that will shrivel them; when paste is done, having removed the upper crust, fill dish with oysters and gravy, replace the cover and serve hot.

Mrs. JAMES MILLER.

Fried Oysters.

Put a piece of butter in a frying pan with pepper and salt to season; heat hot, then put in oysters, thoroughly drained, and fry quickly.

Another Way.

Dip oysters in a batter prepared as for griddle cakes, with, perhaps, 1 or 2 more eggs; then fry in butter and lard, half of each; the true philosophy of frying is to have the fat at a boiling heat before any thing is put into it; if only warm it penetrates, and the food is greasy.

Fried Oysters.

Drain the liquor from 1 can of oysters, beat 2 eggs, dip oysters in the egg, then in rolled cracker, and fry brown in butter and lard, half of each.   F. L. EOSTER.

Scalloped Oysters.

To 1 can oysters, 1 loaf bakers bread, (stale,) remove the crust and use only the inside, crumbled fine; butter a deep tin or earthern dish, and fill with alternate layers of bread and oysters; the first and last layers should be bread; season each layer of oysters with pepper, salt and butter; moisten with the liquor from the oysters; bake ½ hour, and serve immediately.   F. L. FOSTER.

Directions for making Chowder.

Cut the fish in pieces 2 inches square; fry 6 slices of salt pork in an iron pot till crisped; take out the pork leaving the fat; put into the pot a layer of fish, several bits of the fried pork, and a layer of crackers that have been soaked tender in cold water; season with salt, black and red pepper, (onions if liked) and other spices; repeat the process till you have used all the fish required for the chowder; then turn sufficient cold water to cover the whole, and stew from 25 to 30 minutes; put the fish in the dish in which you are to serve it, and keep warm. Thicken the gravy with pounded cracker; add ½ pint white wine or a large spoonful of catsup; garnish with slices of lemon, after adding the juice of 1 or 2. Cod and Haddock make the best chowder. (Rye Beach.)

Mrs. Wm. M. FERRY,
Grand Haven.

To Cook Clams.

Roast in a pan over a hot fire, or in a hot oven, or at a "Clam Bake" on hot stones; when they open empty the juice into a sauce pan, add the clams with butter, pepper and very little salt. (Rye Beach.)   Mrs. Wm. M. FERRY.

To Boil Clams.

Put them in a pot with very little water, and so as to save their juices, proceed as in preparing roast clams, and lay buttered toast in the dish when you take them up. Clams fried in egg batter are a nice breakfast dish. (Rye Beach.)   Mrs. Wm. M. FERRY.

Saratoga Fried Potatoes

Cut nice potatoes into very thin slices, put them into cold water with a small bit of alum added to make them crisp; let them stand a few hours, or over night; rinse in cold water, and dry them with a crash towel; fry them a light brown in boiling fat; add a little salt. (Saratoga specialty.) Mrs. Wm. M. FERRY.

Boiled White Fish.

Taken from Mrs. A. W. Ferry's Cook Book, Mackinac, 1824.

The most delicate mode of cooking white fish:

Prepare the fish as for broiling, laying it open; put it into a dripping pan with the back down; nearly cover with water; to one fish 2 tablespoonsful of salt; cover tightly and simmer (not boil) $\frac{1}{2}$ hour. Dress with the gravy, a little butter and pepper, and garnish with hard boiled eggs. Mrs. Wm. M. FERRY,
Grand Haven.

Boiled Codfish.

Cut the fish into square pieces, cover with cold water, set on the back part of the stove; when hot pour off water and cover again with cold water; let it stand about 4 hours and simmer; fry a few slices of pork, put the fish on a platter, and pour the pork fat over it; then cover with a drawn butter gravy, and serve.

Mrs. J. MORGAN SMITH.

Mary's Fish Balls.

2 lbs. codfish, cover with cold water and set on stove where it will keep hot, but will not boil, for 2 hours; change the water once; then remove the skin and bones, and boil with 12 good sized potatoes; when potatoes are done, pour off the water, and wash all together, then make into balls; sprinkle a little flour over them, and fry brown in a spider with piece butter as large as an egg; add more if necessary.

Meat Balls.

Mince any kind of cold meat, game, fish or poultry; season it well mix with some gravy thickened almost to a paste with yolks of eggs; make into balls, dip in egg and bread crumbs and fry them brown; $\frac{1}{3}$ more lean than fat, or they will not be firm.

Mrs. WORDEN.

Croquets.

Take any kind of fresh meat or fowl, chop very fine, add an equal quantity of smoothly mashed potatoes, mix, and season with butter, salt, black pepper, a little prepared mustard, and a little cayenne pepper; make into cakes, dip in egg and bread crumbs and fry a light brown; a nice relish for tea.

Mrs. GREEN, Louisville, Ky.

Gravy for Fish Balls.

Piece butter the size of an egg, 1 tablespoon flour, ½ pint boiling water; boil a few minutes and add 3 hard boiled eggs, sliced.

COLLEGE AVENUE.

Plain Bread and Cakes.

Brown Bread.

1 cup rye flour, 1 cup graham flour, 1 cup wheat flour, 2 cups Indian meal, ½ cup molasses, 1½ pints milk, 1 teaspoon soda, salt; boil in a tin boiler 3 hours.   Mrs. FARMER.

Portland Brown Bread.

1 quart sweet milk, 1 pint bread crumbs, ⅔ cup molasses, 1 heaping teaspoon soda, 1 pint rye flour, 1 pint Indian meal; steam 5 hours and bake half an hour; makes 2 loaves.   Mrs. READ.

Boston Brown Bread.

2 cups Indian meal, 1 cup rye meal, (mixed thoroughly,) ⅔ cup molasses, 1 cake " Twin Brothers " yeast or ⅔ cup homebrewed yeast, 1 teaspoon soda, mix with warm water, very stiff, a little salt, butter thoroughly a pail, (a 3 quart tin pail.) and put in the bread; fasten the pail in a pot of boiling water, and let the bread steam in this way 5 hours or longer.

Corn Muffins.

1 cup flour, 1 cup corn meal, 2 tablespoons sugar, water to make a thick batter; mix at night; in the morning add 2 tablespoons melted butter, and 1 teaspoon soda; bake in cake rounds.

Johnny Cake.

2 cups Indian meal, ½ cup flour, 2 cups sour cream or milk, 2 tablespoons melted butter, 1 small teaspoon soda, 1 egg, a little sugar or molasses.   Mrs. N. L. AVERY.

Sally Lunn

7 cups sifted flour, ½ cup butter warmed in a pint of milk, 1 teaspoon salt, 1 teacup yeast, 3 eggs; mix and put into shallow pans; let rise 4 or 5 hours, then bake.   Mrs. READ.

Biscuits.

3 pints flour, butter the size of an egg, 3 heaping teaspoons baking powder; make a soft dough with sweet milk.

Mrs. HALDANE.

Soda Rusk.

1 cup sugar, 2 cups sweet milk, 6 cups flour, 2 eggs, butter size of 2 eggs, 4 teaspoons cream tartar, 2 teaspoons soda dissolved in hot water and added last.　　　　Miss MARY McCONNELL.

Muffins.

1 quart sour milk, 3 eggs, 3 teaspoons soda, flour for a stiff batter.

Miss MARY McCONNELL.

Another kind of Muffin.

.1 pint milk, 1 egg, 1 gill yeast, butter size of an egg, salt, flour to make a thin batter.　　　　Mrs. E. E. JUDD.

Another kind of Muffin.

3 cups flour, 1½ cups water or milk, 1 tablespoon butter, 1 teaspoon white sugar, 3 teaspoons cream tartar, 1½ teaspoons soda.

Mrs. HALDANE.

Bunns.

3 cups milk, 1 cup sugar, 1 cup yeast, 2 eggs; let it rise over night; add in the morning, 1 cup butter, 1 cup sugar, ½ nutmeg, 1 teaspoon soda; make as thick as biscuit, let it rise again very light, then roll the dough and cut out the size of a teacup, and lay in pans by the fire while the oven is heating.　　　　Mrs. E. E. JUDD.

Parker House Rolls.

2 quarts flour, 1 teaspoon butter rubbed into the flour, make a hole in the flour and in it pour 1 pint milk, boiled and cooled, ½ teacup yeast, ½ teacup sugar, let them work into the flour, mixed at night; in the morning knead and let rise slowly until noon, then knead and make into rolls, and let stand till time to bake for supper.　　　　Mrs. HENRY S SMITH.

Potato or Squash Griddle Cakes.

1 pint bowl strained potato or squash, 2 cups flour, 3 cups sweet milk, salt, and small teaspoon soda; sweeten if you like.

Miss MARY McCONNELL.

Green Corn Cakes.

1 pint grated sweet corn, 3 tablespoons milk, 1 teacup flour, 1 tablespoon melted butter, 1 egg, a little salt and pepper; fry with lard or butter. Miss MARY McCONNELL.

Johnny Cake.

3 cups of Indian meal, 1 cup of flour, 1 pint of sour milk, 3 eggs, ½ teacup of molasses, teaspoon salt, 2 tablespoons butter, teaspoon soda; bake 1 hour. Mrs. L. E. GRANGER.

Brown Bread.

1 pint corn meal, pour over enough boiling water to thoroughly scald it; when cool, add 1 pint light white bread sponge, mix well together, add 1 cup molasses, and graham flour enough to mould; this will make 2 loaves; when light bake in a moderate oven 1½ hours. Mrs. W. D. FOSTER.

Wheat Bread.

1 quart milk or water, 2 cups potato yeast, pinch of salt, sift sufficient flour in a pan, put in yeast, salt, and wet up at once into as soft a dough as can be kneaded without sticking; knead thoroughly, when light mould and put into bread pans, let it stand from ½ to ¾ of an hour; bake one hour. Mrs. J. MORGAN SMITH.

Corn Bread.

1 pint milk, 1 pint meal, 1 tablespoon flour. 1 tablespoon butter, 1 teaspoon soda, 2 teaspoons cream tartar. Mrs. PIERSON, Ionia.

Graham Bread.

1 pint sweet milk or water, 1 quart graham flour, ½ pint wheat flour, ½ cup molasses, ½ cup yeast, 1 teaspoon soda, a little salt. Mrs. FRALICK.

Squash Muffins.

1 pint sifted squash, 2 tablespoons melted butter, 2 tablespoons milk, 2 tablespoons sugar, 2 tablespoons yeast; mix up stiff at night, in the morning add a very little soda, not more than ½ teaspoon, and flour enough to mould, not too stiff; bake in moulds. Mrs. JOHN W. FRENCH, Mt. Holyoke, Northampton, Mass.

Graham Muffins.

1 pint sour milk, (sweet milk with 2 teaspoons of cream tartar will answer,) 1½ pint of graham flour, 2 large spoonsful molasses, 1 egg, a little salt, 1 teaspoon soda; bake in cups, or in moulds in a quick oven.   Mrs. JOHN W. FRENCH.

French Rolls.

1 pint warm water, ¼ cup lard, 2 tablespoons sugar, ⅔ cup yeast; put lard and sugar into the water, and melt it up with your hand, then stir in a little flour, then add the yeast, after which, stir in as much flour as you can conveniently with your hand; let it rise over night, in the morning add nearly a tablespoon of salt, then mould ½ hour, the longer the better; let it raise until light again, then take a little piece and roll out, and put a little butter on it, and double it a little more than half over; let them rise once more until light, then bake.   For bread, simply in a loaf; it is delicious.

Mrs. PICKERING,

Kalamazoo.

Rice Croquets.

Take 1 quart cold boiled rice, break in 2 eggs, make into balls with flour on your hand, drop into very hot lard, fry brown; serve hot.   Mrs. MATHEWS.

Muffins or Variety Puffs.

1 quart of flour, 1 quart of milk, 3 eggs, ½ teaspoon salt, 1 tea-spoon melted butter; heat gem irons hot before putting in the batter.   Miss FANNY McQUEWAN.

Sally Lunn.

Rub a piece of butter as large as an egg into a quart of flour, add 1 tumbler of milk, 2 eggs, 3 tablespoons sugar, 3 teaspoons baking powder; bake in square tins, and eat warm with butter.

Miss FANNY McQUEWAN.

Potato Yeast.

10 potatoes mashed fine; pour on 1 quart boiling water: when lukewarm stir in 1 coffeecup of sugar (coffee) and 1 teacup of flour: add nearly 1 quart of boiling water: when cool enough, stir in 1 teacup of baker's yeast, or 1 pint of the potato yeast; let it stand several hours in a covered pail in a warm room, then put it in jugs filling only half full, and cork very tight; 2 teacupsful of this yeast will raise 3 loaves of bread.   Mrs. J. MORGAN SMITH.

Indian Breakfast Cake.

2 cups sour milk, 4 tablespoons cream, little salt, 2 tablespoons brown sugar, 2 cups of Indian meal, 1 cup of flour, teaspoon soda.

Mrs. JOHN W. FRENCH.

Muffins.

1 pint milk beaten with 1 teaspoon sugar, a little salt, butter the size of an egg, ½ cup yeast, stir in flour to make stiff batter, a little soda in with yeast, and raise three hours. Mrs. GROUT.

Congress Hall Muffins.

1 quart milk, 1½ lbs. flour; mix well; add ½ teaspoon fine salt, whites and yolks of 3 eggs, beaten separately, and well mix all together lightly, bake in a hot oven half an hour.

Mrs. HENRY M. HINSDILL.

Brownies.

2 quarts sour milk, 2 teaspoons soda dissolved in the milk, 3 tablespoons molasses, ½ teaspoon salt, thicken with graham flour quite stiff: drop on a dripping pan and bake. Mrs. READ.

Corn Griddle Cakes.

Turn 1 pint of boiling water or milk on a pint of Indian meal, add 1 pint cold milk or water, 3 tablespoons flour, 3 eggs well beaten, and 1 teaspoon salt : bake on a griddle. Mrs. FULLER.

Rice Griddle Cakes.

1½ pints solid cold boiled rice, soaked over night in 1 pint of water or milk, 1 quart milk added in the morning, 1 quart flour, 2 eggs well beaten, ½ teaspoon saleratus dissolved in a little hot water, 1 teaspoon salt : bake on a griddle. Mrs. FULLER.

Gems.

2 cups sour milk, 1 teaspoon soda, 2 teaspoons sugar, a handful of Indian meal, one of flour, 1 egg, 1 spoonful melted butter, thicken with graham flour to a stiff batter : bake in gem irons on muffin rings. Mrs. HOVEY.

Graham Gems.

1 pint sweet milk, 1 egg, ½ cup white sugar, a little salt ; make a thin batter and pour it into the cups after they are heated; bake quickly. Mrs. W. A. HOWARD.

Waffles.

1 pint sweet milk, 6 eggs, 1 tablespoon butter, 1 teaspoon salt, flour to make a thick batter.   Miss. FANNIE HOLCOMB.

Drop Fried Cakes.

2 eggs, ½ cup sugar, beaten together, 1 cup sweet milk, 1 teaspoon cream tartar, ½ teaspoon soda, a little nutmeg; flour enough to make it the stiffness of cup cake.   Mrs. FULLER.

Baked Omelette.

Beat the yolks of 4 eggs, and add ⅔ cup of hot milk, a bit of butter, 1 tablespoon flour, salt and pepper,. Beat the whites to a stiff froth, and add them; bake in a buttered dish a few minutes, in a hot oven.   Mrs. FULLER.

Buckwheat Cakes.

1 quart buckwheat flour, 1 teaspoon salt, 4 tablespoons home-brewed yeast or ½ cake "Twin Brothers" yeast, stir in warm water, beat it well; in the morning add 1 teaspoon soda dissolved in hot water, 2 tablespoons molasses.

Rye Drop Cakes.

1 egg, 2 cups rye, 2 cups flour, ½ cup sugar, 1 teaspoon salt, 1 teaspoon cream tartar, ½ teaspoon soda, 1 teaspoon melted butter, 1½ cups milk; bake in "iron clads" ½ hour.

Omelette.

1 cup warm milk, 1 tablespoon melted butter, 1 tablespoon flour, pepper and salt, 8 eggs, yolks and whites beaten separately, mix all, whites last; fry in a buttered spider.   Mrs. GREELEY.

Puff Overs.

2 cups sweet milk, 2 cups flour, 2 eggs, 1 teaspoon butter, 1 teaspoon salt; bake in cups in a quick oven, fifteen minutes; serve hot with sauce.   Miss FANNIE HOLCOLM.

Potato Yeast.

Boil 6 large potatoes in 3 pints water, tie a small handful of hops in a bag and boil with potatoes, when thoroughly cooked drain the water on a large spoon of flour, then mash the potatoes and add to the water with 1 tablespoon of salt, 1 tablespoon of ginger and ½ teacup of brown sugar; when somewhat cooled add 1 teacup of yeast. Keep the whole a little warm until it is light and spongy; cover light and put in a cool place. One cup full of this yeast will make 4 large loaves of bread.   Mrs. M. L. SWEET.

Sweet Dishes or Varieties.

Chocolate Caramels.

½ lb bakers chocolate, (grated) 2 cups brown sugar, 1 cup molasses, 1 cup milk or cream, butter the size of a butternut ; warm the sugar in the oven, then boil all together twenty-five minutes, stirring constantly ; pour into buttered tins and when nearly cold check off with a knife.   Mrs. SWEET.

Molasses Candy.

2 cups molasses, 1 cup sugar, 1 tablespoon vinegar, butter size of a nut, ½ teaspoon soda ; boil briskly 20 minutes stirring all the time, when cool enough pull quickly.   Mrs. J. B. WILSON.

Chocolate Custard.

Take 1 qt. milk and when nearly boiling stir in 2 ozs. grated chocolate, let it warm on the fire for a few moments and then remove and cool ; beat the yolks of 6 eggs and 2 whites with 8 tablespoons sugar, then pour the milk over them, flavor and bake as any custard. Make a meringue of the remaining whites.

                                        Miss McCONNELL.

Russian Cream.

Soak ½ box of Cox's gelatine in 1½ pints cold water for an hour, beat the yolks of 4 eggs with one cup of sugar ; put 1 qt. of milk on to heat, when warm stir the eggs, sugar and gelatine in until the latter is dissolved, let it come to a boil as for soft custard ; beat the the whites of the eggs to a stiff froth, and when the custard is just warm stir them in, flavor to the taste and put into moulds.

                                        Mrs. J. B. WILSON.

Bavarian Cream.

1 pt. cream sweetened very sweet, 3 tablespoons wine, 1 tablespoon vanilla ; after beating the cream up lightly, stir in ⅓ of a box of "Cox's Sparkling Gelatine" dissolved in ⅓ teacup of warm water ; while straining in the gelatine beat the cream thoroughly, add the whites of 6 eggs well beaten ; beat them all together, pour into a mould and let it stand an hour in a cool place ; serve with or without jelly.   Mrs. W. D. FOSTER.

Cream Nectar.

1 lb coffee sugar, 1 qt. water, 1 oz. tartaric acid, boil 5 minutes in porcelain kettle; while boiling add 1 tablespoon of cornstarch mixed in a little cold water, when cool add juice of 1 lemon, whites of 2 eggs, flavor to taste; 2 tablespoons of liquid to a goblet of ice water, then add ½ spoon of soda. The liquid will keep a month if bottled and kept in a cool place. Mrs. M. L. SWEET.

Strawberry Whips.

Whip sweetened rich cream as stiff as possible; fill the glasses half full of the juice of strawberries sweetened and strained, and pile the cream on top, then lay a strawberry on each glass.
Mrs. E. E. JUDD.

Lemon Beer.

9 lbs. sugar, 3 nutmegs, 6 ozs cream tartar, 6 lemons, 3 pts. yeast, 10 gallons water; put 4 gals. water to the sugar and boil it, put in 3 eggs well beaten to cleanse it before it boils, then skim it carefully, turn the remaining part of the water into a firkin, slice in the lemons, grate in the nutmegs, put in the cream tartar, the boiling sugar and then the yeast, stir, let stand 12 hours and bottle up.
Mrs. E. E. JUDD.

Apple Island.

Stew apples enough to make a quart, strain through a sieve, and sweeten with fine white sugar, flavor with lemon or rose, beat the whites of 6 eggs to a stiff froth and stir it slowly into the apples, but do not do this until just before serving, use but little water; serve a boiled custard made of the yolks of the eggs and 1½ pints milk to eat with it. Mrs. PECK.

Charlotte Russe, No. 1.

1 pt. milk, 1 pt. cream; 1 gill white wine, ½ oz. gelatine, 4 eggs; dissolve the gelatine in the milk and let them boil, then take from the stove, add the beaten yolks of the eggs, and the wine to the (thick) cream and beat to a froth, beat the whites to a stiff froth and mix with the boiled custard, sugar to the taste, and flavor with lemon or vanilla; lastly, stir in the whipped cream lightly, line a dish with sponge cake making the pieces adhere with whites of eggs, and pour in the above. Mrs. H. J. HOLLISTER.

62

Wine Jelly.

1 box gelatine, (size marked 1-s) pour over it 1 pt cold water, let stand 10 minutes, add 2 coffeecups sugar and juice and rind of 1 lemon, add 1½ pints boiling water, 1 coffeecup wine; stir until dissolved then strain, put into the mold immediately; this will surely jelly in a few hours. Add the boiling water last of all but the wine.   Mrs. E. E. JUDD.

White Custard.

1 pint cream, 1 pt. new milk, sweeten to taste, beat the whites of 4 eggs and mix all together, put it over the fire and stir all the time till it thickens, take off and stir a few minutes afterward, flavor and put in cups; beat up the whites of eggs and put on top as for floating island.   Mrs. S. L. WITHEY.

Charlotte Russe, No. 2.

1 quart sweet milk, boil, and stir in while boiling 4 eggs, 2 tablespoons cornstarch, and 1 teacup sugar beaten together; when cold, add ½ pint thick cream, whipped; flavor with vanilla. Line a dish or mould with sponge cake and pour in the above
                                                   Mrs. SLIGH.

Cream Candy.

3 lbs. loaf sugar, ½ pint water; set over slow fire ½ hour, 1 teaspoon gum arabic dissolved in 1 tablespoon vinegar; boil, and pull like molasses candy.   Miss ALICE J. FRALICK.

Charlotte Russe, No. 3.

1 quart thin cream, sweeten to taste, set on ice or in a cool place ready to whip; dissolve ½ box gelatine in a little hot water, have ready a sponge cake about ½ an inch thick, baked in a large dripping pan; fit a piece of letter paper nicely in the bottom of a mould, cut with a sharp knife a piece of cake just the size of the top of the mould, measure the depth of mould, and cut cake in strips this width; once in about an inch, gash the top of the cake, but do not cut through. Put this round the side of the mould, then whip the cream, taking off the froth into another dish until all is whipped. Add gelatine and flavor with vanilla, beating well, fill moulds; put on the piece of cake cut for the top and set on ice, or in the winter in a cool place to harden. This will fill two good sized moulds.
                                                 Mrs. MATHEWS.

Sea Foam.

½ box gelatine, cover with water and let stand ten minutes; add 1 pint boiling water, 2 cups sugar, juice and part of grated rind of 1 lemon; when cool, add the whites of 3 eggs well beaten; beat the whole 1 hour in a cool place; to be served with canned fruit.

Miss ALICE J. FRALICK.

Chocolate Caramels.

1 cup molasses, 1 cup milk, 2 cups brown sugar, ½ ℔ bakers chocolate, butter size of an egg stirred with 1 tablespoon flour; boil about ¾ of an hour. ANNA GRANGER.

Lemon Jelly.

To a package of gelatine, add a pint of cold water, the juice of 4 lemons and the rind of 1; let it stand 1 hour, then add 3 pints of boiling water and 2 lbs. crushed sugar; strain, run into moulds and stand in cool place. Mrs. W. D. FOSTER.

Coffee or Chocolate Blancmange.

1 cup strong coffee or chocolate, 2 cups thin sweet cream, sweeten quite sweet, ¼ of box of gelatine dissolved, mix all together, strain, set on ice till hard like jelly; eat with sweetened cream.

Mrs. MATHEWS.

Tapioca Cream.

Soak 1 teacup tapioca over night in milk, then stir in the yolks of 3 eggs beaten with 1 cup of white sugar, flavor to taste, pour on 1 quart boiling milk and stir well; when the mixture boils, stir in gently the beaten whites of 3 eggs. To be eaten cold.

Mrs. J. MORGAN SMITH.

Cornstarch Blancmange. (Prof. Blot.)

Boil 1 pint milk ten minutes; beat 3 tablespoons cornstarch with cold milk, and stir gradually into the boiling milk; boil ½ minute and pour into a mould. To be eaten cold with milk and sugar flavored to taste, or with the following:

CORNSTARCH SAUCE.—½ pint milk boiled, yolks of 2 eggs, and 2 tablespoons sugar beaten together and stirred into the milk; flavor to taste. Mrs. J. MORGAN SMITH.

Arrow Root Custard.

1 qt· milk, 3 eggs, 1 tablespoon arrowroot, a little salt and sugar to taste, flavor with lemon.   Mrs. FARMER.

Ice Cream.

To a qt. of milk, 2 tablespoons cornstarch, 1 egg beaten separately, beat the yolks and starch together, wet in a little cold milk, add the boiling milk till it thickens, not boils, sweeten and flavor to taste, beat the whites to a stiff froth and stir in when you take the other from the fire; to two quarts add one of cream, though less will do.   Mrs. S. L. WITHEY.

Blackberry Syrup.

To 1 pint juice use 1 lb. white sugar, $\frac{1}{2}$ oz. cinnamon, $\frac{1}{4}$ oz. mace, 2 teaspoons cloves; boil together 15 minutes, strain through a cloth, when cool add 1 wineglass of brandy to every pint of syrup, bottle and seal up.   Mrs. N. CARPENTER.

Spanish Cream.

2 qts. milk, 3 cups sugar, 6 eggs beaten separately, $\frac{1}{2}$ box gelatine, 1 gill wine, juice of 1 lemon; put the gelatine into 1 pint cold milk, boil the rest of the milk and pour to it, then add the yolks of the eggs and the wine and 2 cups sugar, bake till a nice brown, beat the whites with a cup of sugar and a little lemon and put on top, put in the oven to stiffen.   Mrs. CROSBY.

Crab Apple Jelly.

Cut the apples in halves, put them in water enough to cover and boil till tender, but not to a mash, strain off the juice through a flannel bag, use a pound of crushed sugar to a pint of juice, boil ten minutes.

Ice Cream.

12 eggs, 2 lb. sugar, 4 tablespoons cornstarch, 1 gallon new milk, cook in kettle of water like custard; flavor with vanilla.
                              Mrs. O. S. CAMP.

Miscellaneous.

Tomato Catsup.

1 tablespoon mustard, 1 tablespoon allspice, 1 tablespoon cinnamon, 1 tablespoon black pepper, 1 tablespoon salt, 1 teaspoon cloves, 1 nutmeg, 1 qt. good vinegar, to 3 qts. pulp.   Mrs. E. E. JUDD.

Cucumber Catsup.

Take cucumbers suitable for the table, peel and grate them, salt a little, and put in a bag to drain over night; in the morning season to taste with salt, pepper and vinegar, put in small jars and seal tight for fall or winter use.   Mrs. STEVENS.

Rich Pudding Sauce.

1 teacup sugar, ½ teacup butter, 1 large spoon boiling water, 3 large spoonsful of wine.   Mrs. S. L. WITHEY.

Pudding Sauce.

1 cup sugar, ½ cup butter stirred to a cream, 1 teaspoon flour, turn ¾ cup boiling water to the flour and boil, then pour over the butter and sugar, flavor to taste.   Mrs. S. L. WITHEY.

Cabbage Salad.

2 eggs, butter the size of ½ an egg, 2 taplespoons sugar, 1 coffeecup vinegar, mustard and pepper ; cook in kettle of water like custard : chop the cabbage and pour the dressing on cold.

Mrs. W. D. FOSTER.

Corn for Winter Use.

Scald the corn on the cob, and cut it off as for drying, put 3 teacups of corn to 1 of salt, pack in jars ; when used, freshen and cook with milk, and season with pepper, butter, cream, and a little sugar.

Mrs. E. M. KENDALL.

Pickled Plums.

1 pint vinegar, 1 lb. sugar, 1 ounce cloves, 1 ounce cinnamon, for every three lbs. plums ; scald together and pour on hot 3 successive days.   Mrs. FARMER.

Gooseberry Catsup.

9 lbs. gooseberries, 6 lbs. brown sugar, put on the fruit and sugar, with a gill of water, and boil slowly for three hours, stiring constantly, 1 qt. good vinegar and boil ½ hour, then add ½ teacupfull of cloves, and the same of allspice, just as you are taking it off. Bottle while hot, and seal. It will keep for years. Plums and Cherries are nice done in the same way.

Mrs. F. M. CHAMBERLIN.

Water Melon Pickle.

10 lbs. water melon rind boiled in pure water until tender, drain the water off, and make a syrup of 2 lbs. white sugar, 1 qt. vinegar, ½ oz. cloves, 1 oz. cinnamon. The syrup to be poured over the rind boiling hot 3 days in succession.

Mrs. AMELIA YOUNG,
Louisville, Ky.

German Sauce.

1 gal. finely chopped cabbage, 1 gal. chopped green tomatoes, 1 quart do. onions, 3 gills white mustard seed, 1½ do. celery seed, 2 tablespoons ground mustard, 2 do. pepper, 2 do. cloves, 2 do. mixed spices, mace, allspice and cinnamon, 1 gill salt, 1 lb brown sugar, 3 quarts best vinegar, mix all together and boil until soft, stirring frequently. A tin or porcelain kettle should be used. The tomatoes should be sliced, a little salt sprinkled over them, and thoroughly drained.

Mrs. F. M. CHAMBERLAIN.

Dressing for Lettuce or Cabbage.

3 well beaten eggs, 3 tablespoons sweet cream, 3 tablespoons prepared mustard, a bit of butter, 10 tablespoonsful of vinegar, a little cayenne pepper and salt, 2 tablespoons brown sugar, put it over the fire and stir until it thickens.

Mrs. F. M. CHAMBERLAIN.

Chow Chow.

1 peck of green tomatoes chopped fine, add 1 teacup salt, let stand over night, strain off in the morning and add 6 green peppers, 4 onions, 1 cup sugar, 1 cup grated horse radish, 1 tablespoon ground cloves, 1 of cinnamon, 1 of allspice, cover with vinegar and cook until done.

Mrs. L. S. LOVELL, Ionia.

Green Tomato Pickle.

1 peck green tomatoes, 1 cup horse radish, 6 green peppers, 1 tablespoon ground allspice, 1 do. cinnamon, 1 do. cloves, 1 cup sugar, 3 pints good vinegar; boil until soft; slice the tomatoes, sprinkle salt over them, and let them stand over night to drain.

F. M. C., Bunker Hill,
Illinois.

Staten Island Peach Pickle.

7 lbs. peaches (a cling best) 3 lbs. sugar, 1 pint best vinegar, ½ oz. mace, ½ oz. cinnamon, ½ oz. cloves; wash and dry the peaches, boil the vinegar, spices and sugar, pour over the peaches and let them stand 24 hours; repeat the second day; the third day, put the whole over the fire and let them come to a boil, when they are done.

Mrs. F. M. CHAMBERLAIN.

Tomato Catsup.

Break up a bushel of tomatoes in 1½ pints salt, ¼ lb. cloves, ¼ lb pepper, ¼ lb cinnamon, ¼ lb allspice; let them remain over night; in the morning place them over the fire, and let boil 3 or 4 hours, about ½ hour before taking off the fire, add 1 quart vinegar; strain through a sieve and bottle immediately. Use whole spices.

Mrs. FARMER.

Pickled Oysters.

1 gallon of oysters; wash them well in their own liquor; carefully clear away the particles of shell, then put them into an iron kettle, pour the liquor over them, add salt to your taste; let them just come to the boiling point, then skim them out and lay in a dish to cool; put a sprig of mace, and a little whole pepper, and allow the liquor to boil some time, skimming it now and then so long as any scum rises. Pour it into a pan and let it cool. When perfectly cool, add ½ pint of strong vinegar, place the oysters in a jar and pour the liquor over them. Mrs. DR. GROUT.

Pickled Purple Cabbage.

Quarter them, put them in a keg and sprinkle over them a great deal of salt; let them stand 5 or 6 days; to a gallon of vinegar, 1 oz. mace, pepper corns, cinnamon, cloves and allspice; heat the vinegar hot, put in a little alum and turn on, leave the salt on, heat and turn on 6 or 7 times. Mrs. THROOP.

Currant Catsup.

4 lbs. currants, 2 lbs. sugar, 1 pint vinegar, cinnamon and cloves.

Mrs. BREWER.

Spiced Currants.

5 lbs. currants, 4 lbs. brown sugar, 2 tablespoons cloves, 2 tablespoons cinnamon, 1 pint vinegar; boil 2 hours or more until thick.

No. 2.

4 quarts ripe currants, 3½ lbs brown sugar, 1 pint vinegar, 1 table-spoon allspice, 1 tablespoon cloves, little nutmeg; boil 1 hour stir-ring occasionally.   Miss FANNIE McQUEWAN.

Chili Sauce

6 large ripe tomatoes, sliced; 2 tablespoons salt, 2 tablespoons sugar, 2 green peppers, little white mustard seed, 2 small onions, a tumbler of vinegar; boil 2 hours; after cooking, strain through a cullender.   Mrs. PIERSON, Ionia.

Cucumber Pickles.

For 1 bushel make a brine that will bear up an egg. Heat boiling hot and pour over the cucumbers; let them stand 24 hours, then wipe dry; heat vinegar boiling hot and pour over and let them stand 24 hours, then change the vinegar and add 1 quart brown sugar, 1 pint white mustard seed, small handful cloves and cinna mon, alum the size of an egg, a little celery seed; heat boiling hot and pour over the cucumbers.   Mrs. O. S. CAMP.

Cucumbers.

A good way to put down cucumbers, a few at a time:

When gathered from the vines, wash, and put in a firkin or half barrel, layers of cucumbers and rock salt alternately, enough salt to make sufficient brine to cover them, no water; cover with a cloth; keep them under the brine with a heavy board; take off the cloth and rinse it every time you put in fresh cucumbers, as a scum will rise and settle upon it. It is not necessary to make new brine every year; use plenty of salt and it will keep for years. To prepare pick-les for use, soak in hot water, and keep in warm place until they are fresh enough, then pour spiced vinegar over them and let them stand over night, then pour that off and put on fresh.

Tar Soap.

4 cakes Babbitt's soap, ½ pint tar, ½ lb pulverized pumice, 1 quart water; boil fifteen minutes; when cool, cut into cakes for use. Good for chaped hands.   Mrs. C. C. ROOD.

To Restore Rusty Black Lace.

A teaspoonful of gum arabic dissolved in 1 teacupful of boiling water; when cool, add ½ teaspoon black ink, dip the lace and spread smoothly between the folds of a newspaper, and press dry with book or the like. Lace shawls can be dressed over in this way, by pinning a sheet to the carpet, and stretching the shawl upon that.

Mrs. F. M. CHAMBERLAIN.

To dress over black alpacas or black worsted dress goods of any kind, sponge with cold black tea, and iron on wrong side.

To Clean Black Ribbon or Silk.

Take an old kid glove (black preferable) no matter how old, and boil it in a pint of water for a short time, then let it cool until the leather can be taken in the hand without burning; use the glove to sponge off the ribbon; If the ribbon is very dirty, dip it into water and draw it through the fingers a few times before sponging. After cleaning lay a piece of paper over the ribbon and iron; paper is better than cloth. The ribbon will look like new.

Moths in Carpets.

Take a coarse crash towel, wring it out in clean water and spread it out smoothly on the carpet, then iron it dry, repeating the operation in all suspected places, and those least used; then, by placing a few crumbs of sulphur under the edges of the carpet, the result is accomplished.

To Renovate Black Silk.

Rub the silk all over on the right side with a solution of ammonia and water, (2 teaspoons of powdered ammonia to $\frac{1}{4}$ pint warm water,) and smooth it on the wrong side with a moderately hot iron, and the silk will present a bright black appearance.

To Remove Iron-Rust from White Goods.

1 oz. oxalic acid dissolved in 1 quart water; wet the iron-rust spots in this solution, and lay in the hot sun; the rust will disappear in from 3 to 20 minutes, according to its depth; or, hold the rusted cloth, wet in this solution over the steam of a boiling tea-kettle; in either case the cloth should be will rinsed in water as soon as the rust disappears, to prevent injury from the acid. Many use this acid to remove fruit and ink stains from white fabrics. When diluted still more, it may be used to remove fruit and ink stains from the hands.

Disinfectants.

The Homœopathic World says, roasted coffee is one of the most powerful means, not only of rendering animal and vegetable effluvia innoxious, but of actually destroying it.

To Cure Ear Ache.

There is hardly an ache to which children are subject, so hard to bear and difficult to cure as the ear ache; but there is a remedy never known to fail; take a bit of cotton batting, put on it a pinch of black pepper, gather it up and tie it, dip it in sweet oil and insert it in the ear; put a flannel bandage over the head to keep it warm; it will give immediate relief.

HINTS FOR HOUSEKEEPERS.

Willful waste makes woful want.

Have a place for everything and keep everything in it's place.

Do everything in it's proper time.

Remember the Golden Rule in the kitchen as well as in the parlor.

Punctuality as well as patience and perseverance, is necessary to the housekeeper.

Do not rob your kitchen of convenient furniture in order to adorn your parlor.

See that your house is well ventilated in winter as well as in summer.

Cleanliness is next to Godliness.

When you have a rule, follow it; guess work fails nine times in ten.

In selecting carpets, choose small figures, they are more durable and furnish a room more.

Tea is good to wash varnished grained wood.

A little milk in the water is good in washing oil cloths.

Old potatoes are improved by keeping them in cold water for several hours before boiling.

Put salt meat into cold water; put fresh meat into boiling water. The more gently meat boils the more tender it is. Allow about twenty minutes for boiling each pound of fresh meat and twenty-four minutes for salt meats.

In making soup put the meat into cold water and let it grow warm slowly.

Put fish into cold water to boil.

Vegetables should be put into boiling salted water to cook, and taken up as soon as done.

Potatoes should steam dry before mashing.

Do not cook butter, it makes it oily.

Oat meal mush is one of the most wholesome articles of food.

In making nice cakes, sift flour and sugar before measuring, and always wash your butter.

Two quarts of wetting will make one hundred and ten 'raised biscuits.

One gallon of Ice Cream will serve twenty-five persons, and more if fruit or jelly is served with it.

1 ℔. of butter equals 1 qt.

1 ℔. of loaf sugar equals 1 qt.

1 ℔. of flour equals 1 qt.

1 ℔. 2 ozs. of Indian meal equals 1 qt.

1 ℔. 2 ozs. brown sugar equals 1 qt.

1 ℔ 1 oz. powdered sugar equals 1 qt.

10 eggs equals 1 lb.

1 gal. equals 1-2 peck.

16 tablespoons equals 1-2 pint.

CULINARY COUPLETS.

Always have lobster sauce with salmon,
And put mint sauce your roast lamb on.

Veal cutlets dip in egg and bread crumb,
Fry till you see a brownish red come.

Grate Gruyere cheese on macaroni,
Make the top crisp but not too bony.

In venison gravy, currant jelly,
Mix with old port—see Francatelli.

In dressing salad, mind this law,
With two hard yolks, use one that's raw.

Roast veal with rich stock gravy serve,
And pickled mushroons, too, observe.

Roast pork, sans apple sauce, past doubt,
Is "Hamlet" with the Prince left out.

Your mutton chops with paper cover,
And make them amber brown all over.

Broil lightly your beefsteaks—to fry it,
Argues contempt of christian diet.

Kidneys, a finer flavor gain,
By stewing them in good champagne.

Buy stall-fed pigeons—when you've got them,
The way to cook them is to pot them.

Woodgrouse are dry when gumps have marred 'em,
Before you roast 'em always lard 'em.

It gives true epicures the vapors,
To see boiled mutton, minus capers.

Boiled turkey, gourmands know of course,
Is exquisite with celery sauce.

The cook deserves a hearty cuffing,
Who serves roast fowls with tasteless stuffing.

Smelts require egg and biscuit powder,
Don't put fat pork in clam chowder.

Egg sauce, few make it right, alas !
Is good with blue-fish or with bass.

Nice oyster sauce gives zest to cod,
A fish when fresh to feast a god.

Shad stuffed and baked is most delicious,
It would have electrified Apicius.

Roasted in paste, a haunch of mutton,
Might make ascetics play the glutton.

But one might rhyme for weeks this way,
And still have lots of things to say,
And so I'll close—for reader mine,
This is about the hour I dine.